The **Fiona Harrold** Coaching Series

Successful Dating

Cherry Claus

7 Steps to finding love

HODDER
MOBIUS

First published in Great Britain in 2005 by Hodder and Stoughton
A division of Hodder Headline

A Mobius Book

10 9 8 7 6 5 4 3 2 1

A CIP catalogue record for this title is available from the British Library

ISBN 0 340 83704 7

Typeset in Stone Serif by
Palimpsest Book Production Limited,
Polmont, Stirlingshire

Printed and bound by
Clays Ltd, St Ives plc

Hodder Headline's policy is to use papers that are natural,
renewable and recyclable products and made from wood grown in
sustainable forests. The logging and manufacturing processes are expected
to conform to the environmental regulations of the country of origin.

Hodder and Stoughton Ltd
A division of Hodder Headline
338 Euston Road
London NW1 3BH

Contents

Acknowledgements   vii

Foreword from Fiona Harrold   ix

1. Clearing the Path   1

2. What Do You Really Want?   17

3. What's Holding You Back?   37

4. Dump the Old, Bring in the New   55

5. Develop Dating Confidence   73

6. Preparing to Fly   93

7. Sustaining Momentum   114

Acknowledgements

This book is dedicated to my very dear friend Raymonde Burnet, a guiding light in my life who died in January 2005; and to my wonderful mother Vivien and her husband Bernard, my brother Andrew and his partner Mary. You have each provided me with evidence that it *is* possible to have a successful relationship when both hearts place love first and are willing to overcome adversity.

With special thanks to Fiona Harrold for her support and encouragement over the years, Sheila at AP Watt for her positive input and Helen at Hodder for her gentle guidance. Thank you to Tony for his help in proofreading and finally, thank you to all the friends and clients I've coached over the years who have shared with me their failures as well as their successes.

Foreword from Fiona Harrold

Finding a boyfriend, girlfriend, husband or wife sometimes seems far harder now than ever before. If this is how it feels for you, Cherry Claus is the coach for you! She has written a brilliant, and brilliantly simple 7 Step guide to finding love. On every page you'll find tried and tested techniques and tips that Cherry has used with her clients to coach them to find the personal fulfilment they yearned for. I have worked closely with Cherry for over five years and seen for myself the tremendous appreciation her clients have for her enthusiastic, caring and common-sense approach. I have even seen her apply her own rules to herself to attract great men into her life! She is a coach who really follows her own advice and walks her talk.

Do yourself a favour and follow her instructions to the letter. *Successful Dating* does exactly what it says it will. In fact, it does far more: it also coaches you to enhance your own self-worth and self-esteem. By the end you'll see yourself as quite a catch, someone others would be downright lucky to spend time with! After all, if you're not enamoured with yourself, why should anyone else be? Do the work, get inspired and get ready for love. And then come visit us at fionaharrold.com and tell us all about your success.

Good Luck and Have Fun!

Fiona Harrold
London, 2005

1

Clearing the Path

What would life be if we had no courage
to attempt anything?
VINCENT VAN GOGH

If you always do what you've always done, then you'll always get what you've always got!

Think about this statement. Do you want your life to be the same three years down the line? No! You want things to be different. Maybe you want to meet the man or woman of your dreams; or perhaps you want to be in a loving long-term relationship, or looking forward to getting married and having children. Whatever end result you're aiming for, unless you take some action and go on a date, nothing will happen!

The fact that you've picked up this book tells me that you have a desire to move on from the way you currently live your life. You've had the courage to admit this to yourself and want to do something to change things. You may not know what to do or how to do it at the moment. You may just need some encouragement. That's okay. Wherever you are on your journey, I congratulate you for starting it – the rewards are so worthwhile.

For the moment, I want you to set aside any worries or bad memories that might be holding you back. Just for now, let yourself daydream about the future. Imagine you already have the relationship you really want. Imagine you are doing all the things you have dreamed of with that special person. Where are you? Take a look around you; what can you see, what sounds can you hear? Enjoy being in this daydream.

Just imagine if the vision you saw were to become real, how much more would you enjoy life? How much richer would your life be? Would this be the final piece in the jigsaw for you? If you could have this relationship, what would it do for your happiness? Spend a few moments thinking about this relationship and the positive feelings it brings.

BE PREPARED TO TAKE ACTION

> You are responsible for your own success!

Each and every journey starts with a first step. I know that there may be some hesitation on your part, possibly some fear and procrastination, but it is important that you've taken the decision to begin.

Having been on this journey, I can assure you that it can change your life in the most positive way if you are open to it. Over the next few chapters I will share my experiences and those of others with you, and provide you with tools and tips that I know work.

But ultimately, *you* are responsible for your own success. However great the coach or trainer, only you can do the work, only you can build your dating confidence and only you can put all this into practice.

Be prepared to be totally honest with yourself and to do all the exercises, which are designed to increase your self-awareness. The more honest you are and the more work you do, the greater the results.

Whether you've been single for a number of years or have just come out of a marriage or long-term relationship, at some stage, unless you want to remain single, you will have to venture out on a date. For lots of people this is a scary process. In fact I know very few who could honestly say that they were really confident at the beginning of the journey.

Maybe you are disillusioned, having been out on dates with no success, and just can't seem to meet the 'right' person. If this rings a bell, then this book is designed to help you too. I was once in that position, so I speak from experience when I say that it will pay you to go back to basics and do some groundwork. Let's face it: if what you've been doing all this time hasn't worked, you have nothing to lose and everything to gain.

Finding someone special to share your life is one of the most rewarding experiences you can have. Don't give up on something you really want. If you do, it will be like giving up a part of you and you're worth more than that. So even when the going gets tough – keep going!

Perhaps you have spent many years giving priority to other things, like your career, pushing aside or ignoring any desire to find someone to share your life with. In my experience, lots of people get stuck like this and let time go by without doing anything about it. They acknowledge that they would like someone to share their life with, but lack the courage to take any action.

Over the next few chapters, I will be encouraging you to build on your desire for change and helping you to increase your confidence. Wanting life to be different, combined with some action, will help you move forward from where you are now to where you want to be in the future.

THE PROOF OF THE PUDDING

Let me share my story. The year 1999 was a challenging one. I had been made redundant, my brother had been diagnosed with brain cancer and I was finding it a bit difficult to cope. Despite much criticism from my then partner, I decided to take a year off to make up my mind what to do with the rest of my life.

Taking the time to find this out was the best decision I ever made. The next move was to end the unfulfilling relationship and take some time to recover. So I set off on my own for a trip around Australia and New Zealand to get in touch with what I wanted from life.

As a result, I created a portfolio career taking in all the things I love to do: coaching, training, developing training courses and travelling. One of the most rewarding parts of my job is coaching. I love coaching people to increase their confidence, move forward, or change careers, and attract or improve relationships.

Now, I believe in walking my talk. My focus had been on building a career I enjoyed and getting myself back on to a firmer financial footing after my year off work. I had been systematically taking steps towards realising one part of the vision for my life and was about to take steps to bring another to fruition.

Whenever anyone asked me what I really wanted I would say, 'I want to move to the country and have a couple of pigs, a horse and a dog.' What I missed out was 'a man would be nice too': this was usually an afterthought. I had got to the stage where I was happy with my life and if a man came along then that would be the icing on the cake but it wasn't essential and I couldn't see it happening. I was so busy doing all the things I enjoyed that I didn't have much time to meet a man anyway.

Two things coincided to change that. The first was that Fiona Harrold asked me to write the dating confidence courses for her website. Shortly after Fiona had written her first book, *Be Your Own Life Coach*, she got so many requests for coaching that she asked me and a couple of others to offer coaching services via her website.

The second thing that changed my life at that

time was that I took steps to realise my vision of living in the country. Eventually I set off in search of my country home with room for two pigs, a horse and a dog.

I drove down to Kent with a friend to look at properties and this step finally made me realise that although I could do it on my own, what I wanted more than anything was to find someone special to share it with. This was the turning point. I decided to follow the steps I'd written about in my courses, the ones I so often coached my clients to take and those I shall share with you in this book.

The result was that I met a wonderful man who asked me to marry him and said he would build me a pigpen when we moved to our house in the country!

HOW TO USE THIS BOOK

> There are no mistakes, only learning opportunities

Over the next few chapters, I am going to take you on an inner journey that at times may be challenging, but will ultimately be worth the effort. Whatever your relationship goal, whether it be to get back into dating or to find the person with whom you want to spend the rest of your life, set aside time to do the preparatory work that will help you to reach that goal. Buy yourself a journal or a notebook to record the answers to the questions given throughout each chapter as well as 'The Work' at the end of each chapter.

The trick is to take things one step at a time. And the first step is in preparation. The more time you can spend in preparing yourself, the more likely it is that you will be successful. It doesn't matter if you haven't dated for years or have never dated. Your starting point is determined by where you are now and your desire to move forward in your life.

If the end result is worth it to you, prepare to take the first step along a journey full of discovery. Before you begin it, however, I want you to adopt the attitude that there are no mistakes, only learning opportunities.

Many of us are comfortable and confident in our own world, whether at work or with friends. However, most people's confidence levels waver more than a little when it comes to dating. So rest assured that if this is you then you're in good company!

Even if you haven't been on a date for years, or don't feel at all confident when you do go out on a date, it doesn't mean that you are 'different', 'abnormal' or a 'hopeless case'. The fact that you're prepared to do something about it says a lot for your determination. I admire your courage for taking the first step.

LET'S START AT THE VERY BEGINNING

What is your starting point? Do you want to get back into the dating scene having been single for a long time? Have you just come out of a relationship or through a divorce and are concerned about having to go through the process of 'finding' someone again? Are you ready for a relationship or do you just want to date? Be honest with yourself. Whatever stage you are at is fine, but be clear in your own mind about your starting point.

If you need more time to get over a past relationship or simply want someone to fill the lonely hours, then think about what steps you must take to ensure that you are fully ready for a relationship. Expecting someone to bolster you up or make you less lonely is a recipe for disaster. Take as much time as you need to get your life re-energised and working. Then put effort into finding someone to share it with.

What Do You Really Want?

Make up your mind to enjoy the journey on which you are about to embark. Don't view dating as a chore, otherwise you'll lack the motivation to sustain the momentum. View it as an essential step on the road to getting what you want. Which brings me to the next question: what do you want?

Spend time thinking about what you really want. Are you looking just to date? Do you want to have some fun without commitment or do you want to find that someone 'special', a potential partner, husband or wife? It's so important to be clear about your goal because this will affect the results you get further down the line.

Be Honest With Yourself

> Before you can be honest with others, you have to be honest with yourself

People often fail to consider properly what it is they really want. Consequently, they find themselves embroiled in an unsatisfactory relationship.

One of my clients came to me because he found

himself in this position time and time again and got himself into situations where he felt uncomfortable and, in his words, 'ended up hurting people'. I helped him to be honest with himself about what he wanted. However, he also needed to be honest and upfront with the women he dated. His desire to avoid hurting them was achieving the exact opposite and making him feel bad into the bargain. So we worked on helping him to be open right from the start. He had not long come out of a serious relationship and fun dating was all he wanted.

He switched from dating women who were looking for commitment to those who were happy just to have a good time for a few months. Consequently, he felt that he was no longer living a lie and was much happier in himself.

Not everyone is looking for a long-term relationship, nor is ready for one. However, before you can be honest with others, you have to be honest with yourself – it can save you a lot of hassle or heartache in the future.

I am not suggesting that if marriage is your ultimate goal, you should necessarily share this on the first few dates! But if you want to settle down, get married and have kids, then to ignore that fact is only going to make it more difficult later on. Be honest with yourself in terms of what you want now and in the future, even if the answer is that you don't really know what you want in the future.

Why Do You Want a Relationship?

In your journal, list all the reasons why you want a relationship or want to start dating again. Think seriously about this and try to come up with as many reasons as you can.

Then look back over your list and highlight any reasons that are in any way negative, such as, 'I want to start dating because I need something to liven up my boring social life,' or, 'I want a relationship because I'm tired of being on my own.'

Now go through each reason and make sure that it is written in positive terms, translating any negative statements into positive ones, such as, 'I want a relationship because I would love to share my life with someone special and would get a great deal of pleasure out of sharing in their life too.'

If there were any reasons on your original list that were written in a negative tone, don't throw them away – keep a note of them as you may want to refer back to them.

IDENTIFY YOUR MOTIVATION

One of the keys to success is to get in touch with your motivation for any goal. Now that you've spent time thinking about what it is you want and why, take a few moments to think how each of these goals will impact in a positive way on your life. What are the benefits of achieving what you really want? How will your life improve? Make a list of these in your journal. Unless you are clear about what you want from the outset, how will you know what to look for and how will you know when you've found it?

Reading through the benefits should inspire you. If it doesn't, rework your list until it does! After all, if you can't come up with reasons that inspire you to take action, you'll hardly be motivated to embark upon a relationship or to go on a date.

TAKE RESPONSIBILITY

An important, even vital, part of finding love is to accept responsibility for what you are about to undertake. At times it can be tempting to blame circumstances, the other person, your ex, your parents or anyone else for that matter, if things don't go how you want them to. When you take responsibility it means that you are then open to learning from your experiences, good or bad. This is a much more empowering place to come from, and realising that you have a choice in this matter will help you to move forward.

Similarly, if you're looking for a man or a woman to make you happy, or to give you the type of life you want, that's going to put an awful lot of pressure on a potential partner. You need to take responsibility for your own happiness. Besides, the happier you are within yourself and the more fulfilled your life is, the more attractive you will be.

As your coach, I want you to choose to accept responsibility for all your pre-dating, dating and post-dating experiences from this point on. While you can't change how others behave or have behaved towards you, you can now choose your reaction to them and your own behaviour.

THE WORK

1. Why bother? Why do you want to embark on this journey? Why have you chosen to read this book and do the work? Before we begin, it will pay you to find the answers to these two questions. When you have done that, ask yourself the question, 'Why is this important to me?' Clarity on this point can make the difference between achieving your goal or not.

2. Room to improve. Buy yourself a journal or notebook and make a detailed list of what, specifically, you are looking to improve in terms of your dating confidence. For example, this might include: being able to relax more on dates; improved rapport; more confident body language; improved eye contact.

3. Where's your starting point? If you had to mark your dating confidence level right now, from one to ten where one is not confident at all and ten is super-confident, where would you be? It's useful to know where you are starting from and great to look back on where you were once you've moved forward! Go through each item you listed in (2) and allocate it a score.

4. Clarify what you really want. Refer back to your account of what you are looking for, whether casual dates purely for fun with no commitment, dates with a view to a serious live-in relationship or dates eventually leading to marriage. Then make a note of all the reasons why that is your aim and the benefits you'll gain from achieving your goal.

5. Create your inspiration. Get in touch with what sort of man or woman you are looking for. Let your imagination run free. Describe their character traits, physical characteristics, interests and personality as well as general details. Make sure that everything you write is in the present tense – not future. To give you a couple of examples:

- He loves travelling and going away for romantic weekends. He loves my body just the way it is and tells me so. He's relaxed and secure within himself. He has a lovely face with strong features, kind eyes and a warm smile . . .
- We've just returned from a brilliant weekend away. She's such fun to be with. I love looking at her; she has the most beautiful eyes and warm smile . . .

Have fun with this! Create something that makes you feel good when you read it.

Key idea

A journey of a thousand miles starts with one small step.

2

What Do You Really Want?

You've got to be careful if you don't know where you're going, because you might not get there

YOGI BERRA

Looking for a relationship without knowing what you really want is like getting into a taxi and, when the driver asks you where you want to go, replying, 'I don't know really, just drive.'

Getting in and riding around for a while is fine. It's a great way to view the scenery and get to know the area. But for an extended period this doesn't get you anywhere. So, even if you are only travelling a short distance or riding just for the fun of it, knowing your destination is an essential step in finding love. The problem is that when it comes to love, not everyone is clear about these key points.

Most people can tell you far more about what they don't like or don't want in terms of dating or relationships than what they do want. There's often a vast warehouse of stored data which can be accessed to answer the question, 'What don't you want/like?' When I'm coaching, it's quite common for a client when asked what they *do* want, to start talking about what they *don't* want. It's often much easier to talk about this because they have had more experience of it! So, let's put this stored data to some good use.

Cast your mind back to a conversation when someone asked you what you were looking for in a man or a woman. If this has never cropped up, that's fine. Just spend a few moments now thinking about what you want.

Did you find your mind wandering from what you do want and like to what you don't? If it's easier for you to consider what you don't want in a man or a woman then make that your starting point. The important factor here is that you begin to get some clarity. But we're not going to spend long focusing on the negative, as I'm a firm believer in the power of positive thought.

BE POSITIVE!

> If you focus on the negative then this is what you will see – you won't notice the positive points

Over the next few days, observe whether your focus is erring towards the positive or negative when you think about what you really want. Make a list in your journal of any negative words or phrases.

Some of the responses I've come across over the years have been: 'I don't want someone: who's not intelligent; who doesn't look good; who's too fat; who's too thin; who tells me what to do; who can't make me laugh; who can't tell me they love me; who's not good in bed.'

If your thoughts or responses have been negative, that's fine. This is not about getting it 'right', it's about finding your starting point and working from there.

Now I want you to do a little exercise. Look around the room you're in, and take a few seconds to notice all the items that are red. *Do not* read on until you have done this.

How many green items did you notice? But you asked me to look for red, I hear you say! The point

I am making is that if you focus on the negative (red) then this is what you will see – you won't notice the positive points (green).

Next, transform each negative phrase you listed into a positive statement. This might be challenging if you have formed the habit of looking at life in a negative light. Consider each item on your list and think carefully how you would express it in a positive way.

For example:

- I don't want someone who's not intelligent = I want a man/woman who is intelligent or with whom I can hold an intelligent conversation.
- I don't want someone who can't tell me they love me = I want a man/woman who is able to express their emotions and tell me they love me.

One of the most important steps in finding love is to ensure that you know the positive side of what you're looking for. If in the past you have started or continued relationships with people you intuitively knew you should have said 'no' to, this knowledge will help.

Daydream to Your Heart's Content

> Visualising is the one of the keys to creating the reality of your future

Clarity about what you want is one of the keys to achieving just that. So don't skip this bit because you think you know what you want. The more you know about this, the more successful you will be.

When you buy a new car or a home, you spend time thinking about it before you start your search. By daydreaming or visualising your goal, you activate your motivation and your desire to take action.

The goal of finding love is no different. You need to activate your motivation in order to take action. This is especially important if you lack the confidence to date. You're going to need all the motivation you can get!

Visualising helps to create the reality of your future, so follow this exercise as often as you can. Just as you did in chapter 1, begin by imagining yourself in the relationship of your dreams. Only this time, make your vision as specific as possible. Even though this is just a dream, pretend that it is happening now. Be present. Bring to mind the things you are doing, what you are seeing, hearing, smelling. How do you feel now you're with this special person? Let your mind wander and enjoy the sensation. Make sure you visualise only positive experiences.

Create Your Wish List

In the last chapter, you described the person you wanted to attract and now you've spent time day-dreaming about dating this person. You should therefore have formed enough ideas to be able to construct a wish list.

Give consideration to each of these topics and write down responses to each of them:

- Character traits that are important to me about my ideal partner or date
- Physical characteristics that are important to me about them
- Shared interests or things in common

Write out a complete list then ask yourself on a scale of one to ten (where one is not very essential, and ten is absolutely essential) how important each one is to you.

COMPROMISE

When it comes to successful relationships, most people will tell you that you have to be prepared to compromise. However, learning to compromise is an essential skill of successful dating too. It pays, therefore, to give some thought as to what you will and won't compromise on.

Return to the list you made in the last exercise. Go through each item and now give it a score out of ten as to how prepared you are to compromise on this (where one is not at all, and ten is totally willing to compromise).

What have you learned? Are there any areas where you might benefit from more compromise or do you compromise too much? If so, ask yourself: 'What would be the impact of altering the amount I compromise?'

GREAT EXPECTATIONS

I have come across many clients and friends who were not willing to bend at all when it came to certain situations. The key is knowing what to be flexible about and what not. This will be different for everyone.

One client of mine, Russell, a man in his early

fifties, was absolutely adamant that he wanted to meet someone in her thirties who was a size ten. Since the break-up of his marriage, he had been dating a lady of this description but sadly the relationship had ended. He had not been having much luck in finding someone else who fitted his description. Such inflexible criteria were hampering his chances of finding what he really wanted, which was a serious long-term relationship with someone with whom he could enjoy life and be himself.

Once we examined his expectations concerning age and size and the beliefs that he had attached to these, he began to see how his criteria regarding age and dress size were limiting his chances of success. A few months later, Russell met a lovely lady who shared many of his interests, had a great figure and who was forty-five years old!

POSITIVE CHARACTER TRAITS

If your aim is to have a successful relationship, then it is essential to give some thought to the positive character traits that are important to you.

The ability to identify these will make the difference between a rocky or a firm foundation on which to build a relationship. Even if it's simply a successful dating experience you want, knowing what these traits are will help you to achieve just that.

So what are character traits? They influence how someone views and responds to the circumstances and situations in which they find themselves. Here are some examples of positive and negative character traits:

Positive traits	Negative traits
Patient	Impatient
Kind	Selfish
Happy	Negative about life
Easy-going	Lazy
Positive in outlook	Quick to anger
Honest	Dishonest
Generous	Mean
Loyal	Disloyal
Humorous	Uncaring
Ambitious	Insensitive
Passionate	Irresponsible
Outgoing	Demanding
Responsible	Critical

A true character trait is generally consistent. If someone has a positive outlook they tend to display that regardless of circumstances. Of course this doesn't mean to say that they won't sometimes feel or express less than positive emotions. But they usually look for the positives in most situations.

So take a moment to ask yourself; 'What positive character traits are really important to me?' You can use the list above or jot down some of your own.

If you've listed more than eight, go through this list and decide which four are most important to you. Then ask yourself why you find each one of these character traits important.

Another of my clients, Julie, came to me with a history of failed relationships. She wrote a list of her most valued character traits, and discovered when she looked back over her past relationships that they all displayed similar negative characteristics. In each relationship there was a glaring absence of her most valued character traits.

Julie had been attracted initially by external attributes such as appearance, sex appeal, successful career, nice home and exciting lifestyle. But she was looking for a serious relationship that would lead to marriage. She had been so focused on outward appearances that she hadn't considered that placing such a high priority on these features might not necessarily lead to stability and happiness. Circumstances can change and often do: people get made redundant, lose their homes and their looks.

We worked on shifting her focus to look at who a man is, not what he has. The shift paid off: she is now dating a lovely man who is kind and caring and, in her own words, 'makes me feel like the best thing since sliced bread'!

WHAT SORT OF RELATIONSHIP?

> Putting some thought into the sort of relationship you want is vital

Until now we've focused on being clear about the sort of person you ideally want to meet. However, if it's a relationship you're after then it's not just the person that you need to focus on, but the relationship itself.

It's critical that you think hard about the sort of relationship you want. Spend a few moments now to consider what is important to you in terms of a relationship.

For instance, do you want just to date and have fun with no strings attached or are you keen to meet someone for a long-term relationship? It's important that you are absolutely honest with yourself about this.

A lot of people prefer to adopt a 'see how it goes' approach, which is fine. It allows you to date someone without too much pressure. However, don't avoid doing some of the work just because you want to hold back and see what happens. If deep down you know that what you're looking for is a long-term partner or marriage, then it's much easier to be clear about what's important to you while you're still single. I have generally found that once people start dating someone, they tend to let this relationship influence their views.

Relationship Values

> Real clarity can help you to walk away from the relationship that you don't want

Before you rush headlong into another relationship, take time to think about what is really important to you in terms of values. Values are the things that are essential for you to be you, that define your character. Although people can share the same values, everyone's will be slightly different because they reflect the uniqueness of that person.

Exploring your relationship values is a very

worthwhile exercise, because the clearer you are about these the less chance you have of staying in a relationship that is not 'right'. So, let's take a brief look at some examples of relationship values:

- Trust
- Kindness
- Passion
- Honesty
- Fun
- Respect
- Integrity
- Freedom
- Friendship
- Intimacy

Go through this list and circle any words that resonate with you, adding any words of your own that are not on the list. Write a description of what each of your values means to you. Ask yourself how important these are to you in a relationship.

Think back over a few of your previous relationships. How many of these values were met? Where were the gaps? What values were missing? It can be quite an eye-opening exercise. However, once you are clear about what is important for you in terms of a relationship, it will help you to walk away from those that do not provide you with what you want.

What if you don't know what you want?

It's important to acknowledge exactly where you are right now. It doesn't matter one bit if you don't know what you're looking for at this precise point in time. It simply means that you're in the process of finding out.

Rediscover your likes and dislikes

Most people form opinions about what they like and don't like from an early age. Some make immediate decisions and others wait and see before giving a verdict either way. Learning from experience forms an important part of many people's decision-making, where they don't decide whether they like something until they've tried it.

In terms of food, most people's tastes expand as they get older and try different dishes. However, when it comes to dating, people are a lot less eager to try something new, even when their experiences have not been that good – it's almost as if a 'better the devil you know' attitude takes over. But just as trying a new dish or type of cuisine can bring many rewards, so can dating someone a bit different from your norm.

It's time to examine your dating likes and dislikes. Maybe you have some that are outdated and you would benefit from getting rid of them. What old preferences or dislikes are colouring your experience of dating? Have you ever been in a situation where you've had a negative experience and said to yourself afterwards, 'I'm never going to do that again'?

I remember, to this day, one of my early boyfriends who was mad keen on football, and every Saturday we had to get home in time to watch *Match of the Day*. This definitely coloured my experience of dating as I made the decision never to date a football fan again! As soon as I discovered a man had an interest in football, I was off!

Had my experience in the first instance been positive, things might have been completely different. I might have sought out football-playing men instead of running a mile. The point is, discovering the reasons for your likes and dislikes is the first step in deciding which ones are currently valid.

Have you made hard and fast rules about your likes and dislikes that could be holding you back from new experiences?

One of my clients came to me after a series of unsuccessful relationships, as she had problems in attracting the 'right' sort of men. She adored motor-bikes and loved nothing better at the weekends than to hang out at biker cafés and events. This was fine when she was in her twenties and into dating. However, she was now approaching her mid-thirties, in the medical profession and wanted to settle down.

She thought that men she met through work were 'too straight' to share her interests and she didn't like 'straight'.

When we examined in more depth what she enjoyed, we discovered that it was the thrill of motor-biking that attracted her rather than the men she met as a result. She no longer wanted to be a 'scruffy biker chick' as she called it. But this was comfort-able and at least she met men who shared the same interests.

Through coaching, she looked closely at exactly what appealed to her and explored new ways to achieve it. Not long after, she traded in her old motor-cycle jacket for a sleek leather suit and went on to meet a charming paramedic who was passionate about bikes!

Do your likes or dislikes need an overhaul? Are you still reacting to past experiences? If so, it's time to let go. Check if your knowledge of your likes and dislikes is up to date and that you are allowing your-self to be open to new experiences.

WHAT IS SUCCESSFUL DATING?

> Until you can determine exactly what you are looking
> for, how will you know when you've found it?

Whether it's finding love or dating successfully, think about your answer to the question, 'What does success mean to me?' What would a successful relationship be like for you? What would it look like? What would it feel like?

There may be different degrees of success. For example, certain features may need to be present for you to feel that a date was successful. It can pay you to be aware of the criteria you employ to judge whether a date was successful or not. Do they need changing? However, it's rather more complicated when it comes to finding a successful relationship.

One client told me that her goal was to have a successful relationship. In exploring what she meant by a successful relationship, she realised that although she used the phrase frequently, she had not thought about what it meant in reality.

Until you can determine exactly what you are looking for, how will you know when you've found it?

THE WORK

1. Start by being honest. Are you ready to have a long-term relationship or is that a step too far at the moment? Perhaps you just want to dip your toe in the water and go on a few dates. Maybe you have reached the stage where you are ready for marriage and want to settle down and have children. Whatever stage you are at, take the time to write this down in your journal. For example:

- I am now ready for a serious relationship, or
- I am now ready to go on a date

What exactly are you ready for? Think of all the things you are ready to do and make a note of them. For instance:

- I am now ready to chat someone up
- I am now ready to make the first move
- I am now ready to smile at people I fancy

2. Define success. Write down in your journal what you mean by a successful date or a successful relationship. It doesn't matter what your friends', your family's or even society's definition is, what's yours? What criteria need to be present for you to feel you have achieved your goal?

3. Positive evidence. Having gone through the positive character traits that are important to you in a relationship ask yourself, 'How do *I* fare when it comes to these?' Examine each positive character trait you are looking for in a partner and consider whether you possess it. What evidence can you produce to prove that you do?

4. Discover your relationship values. Make sure you know what your relationship values are. Once you have identified them, write down your definition of each value and answer the question, 'Why is this important to me?'

5. Keep daydreaming. Now that you are clearer about what you really want, bring this image to life by daydreaming. Visualise sharing time with this special 'person'. If you can't 'see' your perfect partner in your mind's eye, focus on how good you feel when you are with them, the enjoyment you get out of spending time with them, listening to things they say. Bring this vision to life as often as you can and enjoy creating a positive image for your future.

Key idea

Knowing me comes before knowing you.

3

What's Holding You Back?

We cannot discover new oceans until we have the
courage to lose sight of the shore

ANON

Something must be holding you back, because if there were nothing, then you wouldn't have picked up this book! This is possibly the most important area to spend time on if you want to move forward. People give many reasons for not wanting to be in social situations where they might meet someone, go on a date or start a relationship. It's no good ignoring them or pretending they don't exist. The time has come to get them out into the open.

TIME TO GET REAL

Until you can be honest with yourself, a successful relationship will elude you. You may give the impression to your friends or work colleagues that you want a relationship but deep down you're scared stiff. Or maybe you've got a great social life and so imagine that you're not interested in a relationship. Only you know, deep down, what it is you desire.

Over the years I've heard myriad excuses from people for not putting themselves in situations where they might meet someone. These range from, 'It will probably be boring', 'I don't have anyone to go with', 'I'm too busy', 'I don't have anything to wear', to, 'They probably won't be "my sort of people".'

If you want this to continue to be the case, then you need read no further. However, I suspect that you do want your life to be different. By now, you probably realise that unless you're honest with yourself and discover what has been stopping you, you'll be in the same position a year from now.

UNHELPFUL HABITS

It's worth taking a look at what you have done or are currently doing to prevent yourself from meeting or dating people. Habits often creep up on us over the years and become an automatic part of our behaviour without us realising it.

One of my clients identified her habit of rushing home after her weekly game of tennis instead of joining other members in the bar for a drink. At one point she had had a heavy workload, which meant her dashing home after tennis. Soon, she developed the habit of always leaving immediately after her match. Through coaching, she began to look at the consequences of her habits and whether they helped or hindered her goal to meet someone. She realised that this habit prevented her from meeting other members of the tennis club and expanding her social life.

Once aware of this habit, she chose to break it whenever her workload permitted. She is now dating one of the club members as a result of staying behind for a drink in the clubhouse!

So, take a look at your own habits. Which ones are hindering your chances of meeting someone?

DON'T PLAY THE WAITING GAME

Every day there are opportunities to sharpen your dating skills. However, I often hear people say things like, 'I need to lose weight before I go on a date,' or, 'I want to wait until I feel ready.' By placing the day when you meet someone in the future, you'll miss out on the opportunities to meet a man or woman now.

Some people feel that they must first overcome whatever is preventing them from dating, but very often this is just an excuse, another way of procrastinating.

If your goal is to meet someone and have a wonderful relationship, then don't play the waiting game. Don't waste the opportunity you have right now to improve your dating skills. Practice makes perfect, especially if your skills are rusty or limited. The more practice you can get in now, the more it'll stand you in good stead for dating that 'special someone'.

There are others who, even when they have lost the weight or toned those muscles, still do not 'feel ready'. Along comes another excuse or reason why they can't ask a woman out or go on a date. But the real reason is that they're scared. Lurking in the background is a fear and this is what is holding them back.

SELF-SABOTAGE

Are you aware that you sabotage opportunities to meet potential partners or dates? I know people who have become so adept at this that they convince themselves that their reason for not attending this or that event is valid. If this is you, then ask yourself why you're turning down invitations. Of course there are genuine reasons to decline an invite. However, for many single people, it's their underlying fear that makes them do so.

Procrastination

You may procrastinate about getting ready to date for many reasons. They needn't stop you in your tracks though. Once you can identify what you are procrastinating about, you are on the way to eliminating it.

Take a look at what you are resisting and what is causing this resistance. Is it a habit, a belief, a fear or just sheer lack of focus and the fact that you are not giving this area a high priority in your life? If you are procrastinating about doing the very things that would help you to find a wonderful partner, then ask yourself, 'How important is this to me really?'

Sometimes we're not aware of how important things are in our lives. I know from my own experience that it wasn't until I pursued my goal of finding a home in the country that I realised what I really wanted was someone to share this with. Until this point, although I had been open to dating and had even been on a few dates, it wasn't a high priority for me. Once I understood that it was important, I was able to focus on getting what I wanted. I repositioned dating from a medium to a high priority and decided to put more time and effort into achieving my goal.

In my case, it wasn't fear that stopped me; it was simply that I had not made it a high priority. But what if it is fear that is stopping you?

When Fear is the Obstacle

Fear can be a major obstacle in achieving any goal and fears associated with dating are no exception.

The first, and often the most difficult, step is to identify exactly what you are afraid of. I often find that what clients thought they were afraid of turns out not to be the culprit, but something else entirely.

One client, Darren, told me that he was afraid of chatting to women and that this made dating almost an impossibility.

When we explored this further, it became apparent that his fear was not of chatting to women, but of opening a conversation with a woman in a dating context. He had no trouble at all in chatting to female colleagues at work. The fear kicked in when he had to initiate a conversation on a date, when often he just froze and didn't know what to say.

I asked Darren to become aware of how he began conversations with female colleagues. We also came up with opening lines that he felt comfortable using that fitted his personality. He spent time practising these, much like an actor reads his lines until he feels and sounds confident playing a role.

During his normal working day Darren practised starting conversations with female colleagues. He built up a bank of successful experiences in surroundings where he felt safe. And, in no time at all, he was confident enough to use these lines in a dating context.

Get to Know Your Fear

If there is a fear that is stopping you from approaching women, chatting up men, going on a date or having a relationship, then get to know it.

Identify exactly what this fear is and write it down. Ask yourself, 'What impact does this fear have on my life?' Look at this from several angles. What impact does it have on you physically and emotionally? What effect does this have from a practical standpoint? Has it stopped you from saying yes to invites?

Now consider what the consequences would be of overcoming this fear. Think hard about the answer to this question: how would things be different for you? Take a few moments to write down the benefits of overcoming this fear.

PREPARE TO CHANGE

> One of the keys to overcoming your fears is being prepared to change

How much do you want to overcome this fear? One of the keys to overcoming your fears is being prepared to change. For many, the idea of change is uncomfortable. We are creatures of habit and change is often perceived as difficult. However, if you really want to overcome your fears, then you'll need to do things differently and focus on the positive benefits of this change.

What exactly do you need to do differently? Think about this in detail and write it down. In what way does your behaviour need to be different? For Darren to overcome his fear he needed to act differently when chatting to women. The behaviour that he needed to change was his apparent lack of confidence. Darren identified that a change in his posture would make him appear more confident and he adopted a taller, more self-assured stance. What do you need to change about your physical appearance to help you overcome your fear?

Stick With It

> Develop the determination to overcome your fears

Rome was not built in a day. The same applies to you and the changes that you are looking to make in your life. Don't expect instant success or it to continue on an upward trend. Think back to when you were a child learning to ride a bike. You undoubtedly took a few falls. But you picked yourself up and started again. You might have got frustrated, but something kept you going and you were rewarded by eventually being able to ride unaided. Adopt this very same principle, the same determination. Keep your end goal in mind and repeat to yourself the phrase: 'If at first you don't succeed, try, try, try again.' Take small steps and practise these until you're there!

Realise you've already begun your journey. You

don't have to wait until you get to your destination before you announce that you're ready to meet someone. Preparing to date is one of the most crucial stages to successful dating, so enjoy the ride!

At this point, all that is needed is to keep an open mind. You can accept a date or ask someone out at any time; it doesn't have to be 'the one' for it to be a valuable experience.

Do Away With the Perfectionist!

Are your perfectionist tendencies preventing you from dating? Are you waiting until you can afford to take a woman to an expensive restaurant before you ask her out? Or are you waiting until you fit into that perfect little dress or those great jeans before you'll accept a date?

Whatever the reason, ditch the expectation that you or the date need to be perfect before you'll embark upon either asking someone out or accepting a date. Of course you want your date to have an enjoyable evening and you want to look your best. However, when your standards are so high that they prevent you from dating in the first place, then you need to take action.

Julie came to me with very high expectations of what she should wear on a date. She regularly refused dates if she thought that she did not have a suitable outfit to wear. She believed that if she did not look her best, then the man would not be interested in her. Coaching helped her to identify that this was a limiting belief. It went back to a previous relationship where her partner expected her to be 'suitably' dressed at all times. If in his opinion she was not 'appropriately attired', then he would ignore her. After helping her to see that this belief was formed as a result of this experience, we set about changing it.

WHAT BELIEFS ARE HOLDING YOU BACK?

> Negative or limiting beliefs control our behaviour, feed our fears and prevent us from moving forward in our lives

Negative or limiting beliefs are incredibly powerful. They control our behaviour, feed our fears and prevent us from moving forward in our lives.

Sometimes we take on the beliefs of others without realising it. However when that becomes clear, you have a choice: you can continue to allow a negative belief to control you, or do something to change it. In Julie's case, once she had realised that she had taken on her ex's belief and we did some work to transform that belief into one that supported her, she no longer needed to turn down dates because she 'didn't have anything to wear'.

So, what negative or limiting beliefs are holding you back from enjoying dating or finding a long-term partnership?

It can be quite difficult to identify your negative or limiting beliefs. Often they are so ingrained that you don't realise they are there. But clues are often given in the comments you make to yourself or others, and as a coach I always listen out for these.

Here are some examples to help you identify your own clues. See if you recognise any of these. They could be things you say to others or to yourself.

- I'm never going to meet anyone
- I'm too old to meet someone
- I always pick the wrong types
- It's too late for me to meet someone
- There are no decent men left!

Self-Image

Negative beliefs related to self-image can have just as limiting an effect on our confidence about and attitude to dating. And they also damage our self-confidence so that all areas of life become more difficult.

Take a look at the following and ask yourself if these or any similar beliefs are holding you back:

- Men don't find big women attractive
- I'm too thin
- No one's going to fancy me
- No woman's going to find me attractive
- No man would want to go to bed with me

Once you start to identify them, limiting beliefs can appear like hurdles lined up along a racetrack. What hurdles are you placing in your own path? How difficult does holding these beliefs make it for both you and a potential partner?

What Can You Do About Negative Beliefs?

Transform them. Challenge them. Question their validity. Take away their power and replace them with positive beliefs.

The first step is to identify your negative or self-limiting beliefs. Once you have done that, write them down and change them into positive statements. Like this:

- I'm never going to meet anyone =
  I am now open to meeting the perfect man or woman for me
- Men don't find big women attractive =
  There are plenty of men who love big women and I am going to meet one who does!

Often we gather support for our limiting beliefs to prove that we were right. We pay attention to the views of society; we listen to people around us; we read magazine or newspaper articles that confirm our beliefs.

However, these views are often just that. They are *other* people's opinions, experiences and limiting beliefs. You do not have to take them on board. If Roger Bannister had listened to the advice given by the medical profession on what was humanly possible, and others' negative opinions, he might not have broken the record of the four-minute mile in 1954.

Roger Bannister demonstrated the incredible power of self-belief. I am not asking you to break new ground. All you need to do is to look for evidence that what you want to believe is possible and be open to this possibility in your own life.

After the death of her first husband, my grandma spent most of her life on her own until the age of seventy-two when she met and married a lovely man and spent the happiest years of her life with him. She proved to me that it is possible to find love – whatever your age. I held on to this and when people older than me said, 'It's too late to meet someone,' I chose not to take on their belief. I knew that it was possible if you believed it to be.

Where do you find the evidence that what you want to believe is possible? All you need is proof that someone, somewhere, has reached a similar goal. Read inspirational true stories in books and magazines; look closer to home among people you know and those you observe in your daily life.

Here's a word of warning: watch out for the 'buts' that can come in to try to sabotage the evidence. For example, 'But they probably didn't look like me, were not as shy as me, were fitter than me.'

Just acknowledge these doubts and reaffirm your new belief. For example, 'I am open to meeting the perfect man for me. I know that this is possible. I acknowledge that there may be obstacles ahead but I am determined to overcome these and find the perfect man for me.'

THE WORK

1. Listen to yourself. Notice what you say to yourself over the next week. Is it positive or negative? How you experience life is determined by your thoughts and you do have control over them. Become aware of your internal dialogue. Make notes in your journal of any negative or limiting beliefs that you identify. Do you tell yourself, 'I can't', or 'I shouldn't', or 'I should'? Just notice if you do and if so, replace 'can't', 'shouldn't', or 'should' with the words 'I could'. Observe the difference this makes.

2. Transform your limiting beliefs. You have probably been feeding your negative or self-limiting beliefs for years. Becoming aware of your thoughts and what you say to people is the first step towards identifying these limiting beliefs. However, you need to ensure that once you become aware of them, you transform them too. When you do this be sure to keep your language positive, present and in the first person. For example, if your limiting belief is, 'I'm never going to meet someone special,' transforming it to, 'I want to meet someone special,' won't work – it puts everything in the future. It would be better to say, 'I am now open to meeting someone special.'

3. Notice negative expectations. It's hard for those around you to stay positive and supportive if whatever they suggest is greeted with a negative. When you have been looking for a partner for some time and you have not been successful, it's tempting to blame outside circumstances or other people. But often it's your internal messaging that's at fault, casting a negative cloud on all dating possibilities. Predicting negative outcomes to events is counterproductive. Often others, including potential dates, are better at spotting these negative expectations than you are. Ask a close friend to be on the lookout for any negative expectations that might get in your way.

4. What's stopping you? There must be something that has stopped you from achieving your goal or else you would not be reading this book. I want you now to take some time to identify exactly what this is and write it down in your journal using the following sentence:

In the past, what has stopped me from .... is .... Complete this sentence as many times as you can identify responses.

5. Tackle and remove obstacles. Unless you remove these obstacles, they could hamper your success.

This chapter deals with tackling internal obstacles but there may also be practical ones. Sometimes, if you are too close, it's difficult to see a way around the obstacle. However, others may see things with fresh eyes. Who can you ask to offer suggestions on how to remove obstacles? Create a plan to tackle and remove each obstacle and act on it!

Key idea

Identify each obstacle and, like a mountain stream, find ways to flow around it.

4

Dump the Old,
Bring in the New

*Life isn't about finding yourself. Life is about
creating yourself*

GEORGE BERNARD SHAW

If you want things to be different, then you have
to be prepared to change. It's no good blaming
others or circumstances for your lack of success in
dating. Similarly, focusing on the reasons 'why' will
not move you any closer to getting what you ultimately want.

All the hours spent ruminating over past relationships – what went wrong, what you should have
done, or didn't do – will not move you forward.
Even if there are some good reasons as to why things
did not work out, focusing on these now will keep

you stuck in the past. Any future relationship will be different, by simple virtue of the fact that it is with a different person at a different time.

LESSONS LEARNED

> If you don't make a conscious effort to dump old relationship baggage, it can hang around and affect new partnerships at an unconscious level

Every relationship we have, no matter how brief, is a valuable learning experience. By the time we get to our mid-twenties, we have amassed a range of experiences that serve to guide our future choices when it comes to relationships.

Not all of these are positive and some can hinder the start of, or progress in, a new relationship. If you don't make a conscious effort to dump old relationship baggage in the form of beliefs about relationships, associated fears and expectations, they can hang around and affect new partnerships at an unconscious level.

START OFF WITH A BLANK CANVAS

I have coached numerous men and women whose relationships have been plagued because of such relationship baggage.

One client, Sarah, had finally found a wonderful man and was very happy with him. However, she often found herself sabotaging her relationship because her old fear was rearing its ugly head. Sarah came to me out of concern that she might ruin her new relationship. So far she had managed to stop herself from accusing her boyfriend, Richard, of having an affair. But she was worried that her fear would get the better of her and she'd end up saying something she'd regret.

In a previous relationship, her partner of five years had had a series of affairs. Sarah grew more and more suspicious and distrustful of him until finally he broke off their engagement.

Unfortunately, the fear caused by this experience had never left her. Every relationship she'd had since then was plagued by distrust. After a lot of work to let go of the past and learn to recognise and build trust, Sarah was able to move forward and enjoy her relationship with Richard. She tells me she is 'far happier now than [she's] ever been'.

So, what do you need to let go of in order to start

with a blank canvas? The past can have a powerful hold on us. Take a few minutes to think back to past relationships and make a note of any negative feelings or beliefs you think you might be carrying.

ACCEPTANCE

> The very first step towards making any change is to identify what you want to change or get rid of

If there are parts of you that you want to change, you can only do this if you accept that they exist in the first place. Be honest with yourself.

The first step is to identify what you want to change or get rid of. Go ahead now and make a list of all the negative qualities you'd like to change or dump before starting a new relationship.

I know that people can find this sort of task difficult, so here's a list of some items that tend to crop up on the lists of both men and women:

Negative Qualities to Dump

- Jealousy
- Mistrust

- Anger
- Criticism
- Being negative
- Sarcasm
- Avoidance
- Keeping score
- Making accusations
- Intolerance

If you have found yourself exhibiting any of the above in previous relationships, please do not blame yourself. It serves no purpose and might make you feel worse, which is not going to help you to move forward! Simply acknowledge that these are behaviours that you have exhibited in the past, which you want to eliminate, reduce or change in the future.

LET GO OF BLAME

Blaming yourself, your previous partners or anyone else, for that matter, for any of your negative qualities is counter-productive to finding love. Holding on to blame keeps you stuck and will affect your progress in the future. When you are ready to let go, here's an exercise to try.

Write out on a single sheet of paper:

> *I .... [your name] am now ready to let go of*
> *blaming .... [myself/ or person's name].*
>
> *I now release .... [myself / person's name]*
> *from any blame for .... [describe the event]*
> *and I now value this past experience.*

Repeat this process for whatever you need to let go of.

Take your piece(s) of paper and put them on a real fire (taking care to apply all safety precautions). If you do not have access to a real fire, put the paper in a fireproof container outside, away from anything flammable, and burn it, again applying all safety precautions. Watch as the flames envelop and eliminate your piece of paper along with your blame. Do this as many times as you feel is necessary.

SET YOURSELF FREE

One obstacle that can threaten your self-esteem and your future happiness is a lack of forgiveness. If you've blamed yourself for the way previous relationships have turned out or the way you have handled them, then it is important to forgive yourself. Maybe you need to forgive someone else as well.

Whoever you need to forgive, doing so will set you free to live the life you want. This does not mean that you should forget what happened, but that you release any emotional attachment to what happened so that you are free to move on. Releasing any 'ties' that bind you to either the person you used to be or a previous partner is an important step in preparing for a new relationship.

Use a simple affirmation such as: 'I forgive myself for ...... or I forgive .... [person's name] for ....' Say it regularly for as long as it takes for you really to believe it. This can be extremely powerful. Try it!

WHO DO YOU WANT TO BE?

> Choose to be the person you want to be; it's never too late to change

Once you have eliminated any blame attached to your negative qualities, take another look at them and decide what you need to do in order to change or get rid of them.

Having decided what you don't want to be in future, you need to decide what you want to replace these negative qualities with. For example:

- I want to replace jealousy with trust
- I want to replace criticism with acceptance

How will you need to handle or react to things differently in future? Is this something you can work on outside a relationship? One of my clients worked on improving her tolerance by deciding not to react in supermarket queues! She used to get really worked up when the queue she was in was not moving as quickly as the one next to her. This intolerance showed up elsewhere in her life and often reared its head in relationships. After a focused effort proved that she could increase her tolerance, she began to feel much more relaxed and in control of her life. The benefits extended way beyond supermarket queues!

If there is a negative quality you would like to change try this three-step process:

- Identify what you can do to make a little progress. Choose something that will be relatively easy
- Continue to add small challenges to see how far you can go
- Reward yourself for any progress, no matter how minor

As long as there's an improvement from the way you would have reacted in the past then you've made progress! Choose to be the person you want to be; it's never too late to change.

CHOOSE TO LIVE IN THE PRESENT

> It is by choosing your reactions, behaviours, beliefs and attitudes in the present that you can change the future for the better

You can only live in the moment; you cannot alter what has happened in the past, so avoid wasting energy that can be used for more positive things.

If you tend to dwell on the past, I want you to make an agreement with yourself that from now on, you will live in the present. Every time you catch yourself mulling over what went wrong in a previous relationship, what you did or didn't do or should have done, say to yourself: 'Stop! The past is another country and I don't live there any more!'

Focus your attention on how you can improve today and the changes you need to make to ensure your future is brighter.

DUMP EXPECTATIONS

It's one thing dealing with your own relationship baggage but what are your thoughts concerning other people's baggage? One phrase I often hear is, 'I don't want someone with a load of baggage.' Almost everyone over the age of twenty-five has had some negative experiences in their life. Whether they hold on to those experiences and allow them to affect the present is another matter. 'Baggage' can mean different things to different people. For some, it is enough to doom a relationship from the start, while for others it is an inevitable part of being alive. Ask yourself what your definition of baggage is.

Check whether you expect that a person is bound to have 'baggage' if they have been through a difficult divorce, a series of unsuccessful relationships or a traumatic experience in the past. A negative expectation could prevent you from entering into a wonderful relationship.

Chloe came to me to help her when she experienced problems in dating again after a traumatic divorce. She had recently had counselling to help her get over her divorce and felt she had dealt with her 'baggage', as she put it. However, what she hadn't realised was that, because of her experience, she now had an expectation that men who had been through a difficult divorce had 'baggage' too. I pointed out that this wasn't necessarily the case and we examined what Chloe meant by 'baggage' and what she was afraid of.

We explored ways in which she could obtain the

information she needed to determine whether she was comfortable entering into a relationship. She agreed to withhold her expectation concerning 'baggage' and allow for the possibility of that person having moved on. To her delight, she discovered that removing this expectation allowed her to relax and get to know the man she had just started dating. With that initial barrier removed, Chloe is now enjoying a loving and supportive relationship.

Before you throw yourself into any relationship, it is prudent to be aware whether the person is 'emotionally available'. For example, are they holding on to past relationship experiences that prevent them from being available for a new relationship? Unfortunately, you only find this out once you get to know them. This is one of the reasons why I would recommend waiting a while before getting intimately, i.e. sexually, involved with someone.

Spending time getting to know someone will allow you to discover if they have dealt with any negative feelings and are at a stage where they can move on in their life. Just as you want to dump some of your negative qualities, accept that someone else may have done the same. Removing the negative expectation associated with relationship 'baggage' will allow you to see the real person.

EXAMINE YOUR STANDARDS

How have your standards been formed? By past relationships or dating experiences? Have you taken ideas from family, friends or colleagues and used these to create your own standards? In other words, how much are they your own standards and how much are they borrowed from or imposed on you by others? Close examination of your standards can provide a fascinating insight into what you really want.

I asked one of my clients from an Asian background to look at this. Once he did so he realised he had been adopting the standards he thought his parents wanted. They were not what *he* wanted at all.

Having identified his standards, he could see those that presented obstacles and affected his success in finding a woman. I asked him to separate those he felt he had adopted because of his parents and those he would have set down anyway. We explored whether he knew for certain the views of his parents. He discovered that he had made many assumptions and decided to find out what the real story was.

He was delighted to discover that his parents agreed with him on most things and it turned out that many of his assumptions about their standards had been incorrect. He returned to dating in the knowledge that he was being true to himself.

Until you examine your standards, how you arrived at them and how useful they are, you can't decide whether any of them might form obstacles. Are your standards up to date or are they out of date? What standards are you setting for yourself or a potential date now? Do they help or hinder you?

High standards can sometimes be a barrier to finding what you want when dating. People often say to me, 'Well, I have to have standards and I'm not willing to drop them.' That's great; just make sure they include what is really important to you and don't turn them into totally inflexible criteria.

ALLOW YOURSELF TO BE DIFFERENT

If you could wipe the slate clean and start afresh, how would you be different? What positive qualities would help you to improve your dating or relationship skills?

Give yourself time to think this through properly. Take an objective look at yourself. Don't criticise or judge yourself; this is a time to look ahead.

To give you a head start, let's take a look at some qualities that would generally enhance relationships. The explanations given are not definitions, they are just suggestions.

Adaptability

This is the ability to adapt the way you approach different relationships and work with your chosen partner to create the relationship that you want.

Adaptability may also include being able to 'go with the flow'. If you have a tendency to control situations or want things to go 'your way', ask yourself what could be gained by trying things differently.

It's important that you decide what adaptability means for you. What will knowing that you are adaptable do for your dating confidence?

Acceptance

This includes acceptance of yourself and others. If you have a tendency to criticise yourself and or others, then developing acceptance will reap big rewards.

Criticism, either spoken or internalised, affects your self-esteem and has a negative impact on relationships. If you are serious about wanting a successful relationship, then cut out the criticism.

Criticising yourself in front of your date will do you no favours in creating a positive impression. Even if you do not voice these criticisms, they are still noted by your subconscious and add to the pile of negative thoughts that damage your self-esteem and confidence.

Similarly, if you tend to cast a critical eye over other people or focus on the negative aspects of a situation, this too can have a detrimental effect on your dating success.

Being negative is not going to stop overnight. If you want to become more accepting, start by recognising the reality of the situation. Accept that you are focusing on the negative and look for ways to balance this out. The more you look for the positives, the more positives you'll find.

Self-Trust

How many times have you doubted your ability to make good judgements with regard to relationships? If you constantly tell yourself that you can't be trusted to make good decisions, you are in effect determining the future. Inevitably, you will make a few decisions that you perceive to be 'not good', which, then confirms your belief, and the situation becomes a self-fulfilling prophecy.

Trusting yourself to make good decisions is such an important part of successful dating. If you have formed the belief that you don't trust yourself, then it's time to change it.

Start by recording all the times that your trust in yourself to make good decisions has paid off. They don't have to be connected with dating, just look for evidence of your trustworthiness. You have probably made hundreds of good decisions in your life and not paid any attention to them before!

MAKING GOOD DECISIONS

You have a lifetime of experience in decision-making and have been perfecting this skill for years. Yet many people express concerns about making the 'wrong' decision when it comes to dating and relationships. There are no 'right' or 'wrong' decisions. Whatever decision you make is the right one for you at the time. Whatever decision you make is a learning opportunity.

THE WORK

1. **Out with the old.** In order to make any change, you need to know exactly what it is you want to change. Make a list in your journal of all the things you want to change about yourself. They could be characteristics you don't like or behaviours you would rather not display. Go through the list and select the three you would most like to change. For

each, complete the following sentence:

I now let go of the need to be...............e.g. impatient.

2. In with the new. For real change to take place, you need to replace your old behaviour, attitude or belief with a new one. For each thing you want to change, record in your journal what you intend to replace it with:

From this point forward I choose to be .....e.g. more tolerant.

3. Focus on change. Changes can only take place when you actively focus on making them. Remind yourself daily of the 'new you' by reading the positive affirmations or sentences you created in (2). Use Post-it Notes in your car or on your computer to remind you to focus on what you want to change.

4. Notice your progression. Change takes time. Don't expect yourself to make changes overnight. Little by little, progress will emerge. Awareness is the key to success. The best illustration of awareness and change is the story about a man who walks down a road and falls down a hole; he pulls himself out and thinks, How did I fall down there? The next day he takes the same road and falls down the same hole.

This time he thinks, I know how I fell down here. The third day, taking the same road, he avoids the hole and on the fourth day he decides to take a different road altogether.

5. Give yourself encouragement. Accept that change, especially personal change, is sometimes slow. You may fall down a few 'holes' before picking yourself up and starting again. When that happens, encourage yourself, just as you would encourage a child learning to walk or ride a bike. Encourage yourself to continue and remind yourself of how well you're doing or how good you will feel when you've made the change.

Key idea

Keep right on to the end of the road; it will be worth it when you get there.

5

Develop Dating Confidence

Courage is not the lack of fear. It is acting in spite of it

MARK TWAIN

One of the most important steps you'll ever take in preparing for any goal in life is to ensure your confidence levels are as high as they can be.

Lack of confidence can prevent you from taking action and this is particularly so with dating confidence. Lack of confidence can often hamper a person's ability to take the plunge and ask someone out; attend social functions; go on a date or even accept a second date. It's such an important issue that I've dedicated a whole chapter to this subject alone.

WHAT IS DATING CONFIDENCE?

Dating confidence could be summed up as: confidence in your ability to take action and connect with others in a loving and meaningful way; confidence in your ability to trust yourself to make good decisions; the belief that you can cope with the challenges of dating; and the ability to handle rejection.

Let's explore this a little further.

Confidence in your ability to take action means that instead of just thinking and talking about it, you take steps towards achieving your goal. If your goal is to find love, then this means being proactive and taking whatever steps are necessary to ensure that you succeed. These might include: doing work on yourself; updating your image; improving your dating skills; joining clubs or dating agencies; and actively seeking out ways of meeting people.

Dating confidence is also about being able to connect with others in a meaningful and loving way. This means you overcome any fear and have the confidence to interact with people on a one-to-one and group basis. You trust in your ability to connect with another in a way that works for both of you. As a relationship develops, you are able to connect with your partner in a loving way and express your feelings.

Dating confidence also encompasses trusting yourself to make decisions. It involves not placing any judgement on decisions made and accepting that all decisions are based on the information available to you at the time.

How Do I Develop It?

> Dating confidence is developed by your willingness to take action despite any challenges you may have to overcome

Dating confidence does not come about through being 'good' at dating or relationships. Dating confidence is developed by your willingness to take action despite any challenges you may have to overcome. It is developed as a result of your determination to do whatever it takes to get to where you want to be. It's based on taking action, step by step. The more steps you take, the more your confidence will grow.

RISING TO THE CHALLENGE

To be truly confident, you need to develop the belief that you can cope with the challenges of dating. These are going to be different for each person; they are whatever *you* perceive your challenges to be.

Here are some of the challenges mentioned to me by clients over the years:

- Knowing what to wear
- Going to social events on my own
- Joining a dating agency / singles club
- What do I say?
- How do I start a conversation?
- How do I keep a conversation going?
- Knowing how much information to disclose
- Knowing when to move on to the next stage – whatever that might be

You may identify with some of these challenges or you may have totally different ones. Either way, take a few moments to pinpoint your dating and relationship challenges.

Make a list of these. When you've finished, go back and grade each challenge with your level of confidence in dealing with it, using the following scale:

1 = No confidence whatsoever
2 = Not very confident at all
3 = Fairly confident
4 = Confident
5 = Really / highly confident

Take a Closer Look

Now that you've identified your challenges, let's take a closer look at what could be behind them. Look for clues in the language you use. Notice the labels you give to events or experience. I often catch clients saying, 'The date was a complete disaster,' or, 'I'm no good at chatting up women.' When we explore their statements further, the reality usually turns out to be a lot less dramatic. Perhaps the date didn't go the way they wanted it to, or they find it difficult chatting up women. Using words like 'complete disaster' or 'I'm no good' just adds to their negative image and does nothing for their dating confidence. To break this negative thought pattern, I sometimes ask them to tell me three things that were positive about the date or situation. They can usually find something.

In building up your self-confidence, it's important to avoid dramatising situations and try to find more realistic labels. If you want to become more confident, positive or optimistic, make a conscious effort to look for the positives in any given situation. The transformation won't happen overnight but keep practising and eventually you'll get there.

Avoid Negative Predictions

Concentrate on creating positive scenarios in your mind by imagining how you would like to be, not what you fear you might be

Just because you've had one or even a few bad experiences when dating, don't assume things will always be bad. Even if you got nervous on a date or, in your eyes, made a 'hash of things' it does not mean that you will react in the same way every time. You are a 'work in progress'. If you have set yourself a goal of becoming more confident, you'll be taking steps to improve your confidence on a daily basis. This will have a beneficial effect on the way you react in the future.

Your imagination can either work for or against you. Don't let it work against you by imagining a negative outcome for a date or a relationship. Concentrate on creating positive scenarios in your mind by imagining how you would like to be rather than what you fear you might be. And allow yourself to imagine your future as you want it to be. This is especially important if you have been dating for a few years without success. Don't entertain thoughts like, 'I am never going to find anyone' or, 'Whatever relationship I have will probably go wrong'. Negative predictions will prevent you from finding what you want.

Overcoming Challenges

Start by taking a look at one of your challenges. Ask yourself: 'What would be the benefits of me overcoming this challenge?' Give yourself worthwhile reasons for doing the work. Make a note of them in your journal. What impact would this have on your confidence when dating?

For each challenge, make a list of at least six things you could do to tackle it. For example, if one of your challenges is feeling confident about what to wear on a date you could:

• Enlist the help of a professional image consultant
• Go to a store and ask a personal shopper to advise you
• Buy a book on the subject

- Take a friend whose opinion you trust shopping with you
- Go through your wardrobe, put together some options and get a friend of the opposite sex to give you their opinion on which outfit is the most suitable
- Give each outfit you try on a 'confidence rating'. If there's nothing in your wardrobe that makes you feel really confident, then go and buy something!

Once you have identified all the possible options for overcoming your challenge, decide which you would be prepared to take. You might choose the easiest, cheapest or simply the one that appeals most. Whichever option you choose, make sure it will assist you in moving towards your goal. Ask yourself what the very first action step you need to take to overcome your challenge is.

Using the example of what to wear on a date, if you decided that seeing an image consultant would help you to feel more confident, then the very first step might be to ask your friends and colleagues whether they know of an image consultant, and do some research into the area.

The smaller and simpler you make the steps, the easier it is for you to progress, and before you know it you'll be well on your way to achieving your goal!

ADOPT A POSITIVE ATTITUDE

> You can choose to have a positive attitude by choosing positive thoughts

A positive attitude goes hand in hand with high levels of self-confidence. With the right attitude, you can succeed at almost anything and since attitude is nothing more than a collection of thoughts, which can be changed, you can choose to have a positive attitude by choosing positive thoughts.

I will be honest with you, though: changing your attitude is going to take time. If you have focused for years on what's not right or not working, then don't expect that to change overnight. But change is possible, with effort.

Susan, a senior manager in a blue-chip company, came to me with a 'glass half empty' attitude that she knew was holding her back. I gave her an affirmation that specifically targeted her areas of concern. Just two weeks later she reported that already three work colleagues had commented on her change in attitude and she herself felt more positive than she had done in years.

Positive Affirmations

Positive affirmations are a wonderful tool for developing and improving confidence and are invaluable in helping to develop a positive attitude. I use affirmations a lot in my coaching practice and design personal affirmations for clients. But designing your own affirmations is a straightforward process.

Positive affirmations are statements that you either believe or strongly desire to be true. To be effective, they need to be:

- Present
- Personal
- Positive

You must express your affirmations in the present tense. For example, 'Every day in every way I am becoming more confident,' not, 'I want to be more confident.'

Affirmations, positive and negative, appear in our everyday language without us even realising it. They pop out in our conversations with people. For instance, you might catch yourself saying to a friend,

'I'd love to meet someone who shares my interests,' or, 'I never meet any decent men.'

Neither of these affirmations is helpful. The first puts your desire in the future and the second is a negative statement that may hamper your chances of meeting anyone.

Your conversations with people are an ideal opportunity to hear yourself positively affirming your future. For example, 'I am now open to meeting someone who shares my interests,' or, 'I'm now open to meeting the right man for me,' or, 'From now on, I am going to look upon everything as an opportunity to improve my dating skills and focus on finding what I really want.' If the person you are speaking to is a little cynical, or has limiting beliefs of their own, you might have some convincing to do. However, defending your intentions or beliefs is a wonderful way to reaffirm them!

Affirmations also need to be in the first person; in other words: 'I now see the positives in every situation.' Affirmations on behalf of other people, such as, 'Simon is now falling in love with me', will not work!

Finally, make sure that your affirmations are always expressed in the positive. For example, 'I am a confident and dynamic woman.' If that's going a bit too far and you can't quite bring yourself to say your affirmation in these terms, then you can express your desire for something. For example, 'I am determined to have plenty of self-confidence,' or, 'My strongest desire is to meet the woman of my dreams.'

Positive affirmations serve as wonderful motivators and affirm your desire to achieve your goal.

Here are some really useful affirmations you might like to try. Choose whichever feels right for you, combine them or alter them keeping in mind the 3 'P's: present, personal, positive.

- I love and approve of myself
- I now choose to focus on the positives
- I am perfect just the way I am
- I now choose to connect with positive people
- I think, act and talk confidently at all times
- I am open to meeting the perfect partner for me
- I am becoming more and more relaxed when talking to women/men
- I now trust my intuition
- I communicate with confidence
- I am worthy of finding the love of my life
- Every day in every way I am getting better and better

Positive affirmations are useful for reprogramming any negative or limiting beliefs. For positive affirmations to work, however, you need to use them, and the more you do so, the quicker they will work. You can either say them aloud when you're alone, or think them quietly on your way to work, in the lift or standing in the supermarket queue. Just as negative beliefs have been constantly reinforced, you need to reinforce your positive affirmations continuously.

If you have any doubts about how effective affirmations can be, especially when spoken out loud, think of the way athletes use them. Take the New Zealand rugby team's 'Haka'. This ancient Maori dance and incantation allows them to become totally focused on the task at hand and puts them into a very strong and fired-up state.

Use this same principle to get yourself into a confident state whenever you need to motivate yourself to do something. An affirmation I have used successfully in the past is: 'I am a confident and dynamic woman and I am determined to enjoy myself tonight.' It worked a treat when I went along to social functions I wasn't particularly looking forward to!

Say your affirmation aloud at every opportunity. Do it in front of the mirror and see what a difference it makes to your behaviour and your attitude about yourself or the situation. In the self-confidence stakes, you are the only one who can make a difference.

Building a Solid Base

One of the most important things you can do for yourself in life is to develop high levels of self-esteem, which act as a solid foundation on which to build. This means that when your confidence takes a battering, which happens to each and every one of us at times, it doesn't rock your foundations.

Confidence levels rise and fall depending on the situation you find yourself in and what you perceive about your ability to cope with that situation. I have many clients who are extremely confident in their working lives, but whose confidence levels take a dive when it comes to relationships. There is no magic formula to change this. However, there are some steps you can take to help to improve the situation that I'd like to share with you.

Get To Know Yourself

Knowing what your good points are and being able to acknowledge them is an essential step in creating that solid foundation. This is not about blowing your own trumpet, but about simply acknowledging yourself, to yourself, for yourself. Look at your good points, the things you like about yourself.

Take a few moments now and make a list in your

journal of all the things you like or appreciate about yourself. Make sure that you write each point in the first person. To help you, here are some aspects you might like to consider:

- Your physical appearance   e.g. I have nice eyes
- Your character traits   e.g. I am patient
- How you treat others   e.g. I am kind
- Your good points   e.g. I am fun

Even if you find this difficult at first, I urge you to continue. I have had clients who struggled to write down ten points. But, once they really started to think about themselves, they identified things that they had never considered before. They said things like: 'For the first time in my life, I've realised that I'm actually not that bad,' or, 'It's really helped me to focus on the positives,' or 'I never thought I'd go beyond fifty, it's really boosted my confidence!'

It's rare that we give ourselves the opportunity to have a positive review. Most people focus on what they don't like about themselves, so it's great to redress the balance.

If, when doing this, you came across anything you felt you couldn't write down because you are not like that 100 per cent of the time, consider adding the following:

- mostly   e.g. I am mostly punctual
- nearly always e.g. I am nearly always kind

AREAS FOR IMPROVEMENT

By doing exercises where you look at what you like about yourself, invariably you'll think of things you don't like. That's okay. Fully accepting yourself 'warts and all' allows your confidence to grow and strengthens your core base.

The more you can accept yourself as you are now, the less chance criticism has of damaging your self-confidence. However, I want to make one thing clear: accepting yourself doesn't mean that you don't want to change yourself, it just helps to keep the inner critic at bay.

Remember that list of negative qualities to dump you made in chapter 4? Use that as the starting point to identify traits you want to change about yourself. Then, take the one quality you'd most like to change and instead of criticising yourself for being this way remind yourself that you are in the process of becoming different. For example:

- I acknowledge that I am impatient and I am working on becoming more patient as each day passes.

- I accept that I am intolerant at times but I am determined to change and am consciously working at adopting a more tolerant approach.

In this way, you can quieten your inner critic.

MAKE READJUSTMENTS

Each new experience, whether you perceive it as positive or negative, is an opportunity for you to learn. Every day, the thoughts you create and the actions you take, move you towards or away from your goal.

It may surprise you to know that in getting from A to B, aeroplanes are off course most of the time. The pilot is always making correctional moves to keep the plane on course. Dating is very much like flying in this respect, because although you may know where you want to go, your course to finding love may require lots of adjustments before you arrive at your destination. The skill lies in making these adjustments without getting disheartened and giving up.

THE WORK

1. Be kind to yourself. Treat yourself as you would your best friend. You wouldn't criticise your best friend all the time, so don't do this to yourself! Be gentle on yourself. Allow yourself not always to get it 'right'.

2. Act as if. Actors learn to act 'as if' professionally. However, almost everyone, including you, has at some stage acted 'as if'. Have you ever faked an injury or pain to get out of doing something? Pretended that you were cross with a child while smiling on the inside? You can apply the same acting abilities when it comes to confidence. Act 'as if' you were the most gorgeous woman in the room, act 'as if' you are a charismatic and confident man. Pretend to be you who want to be.

3. Give compliments. How often do you give yourself a compliment? How often do you give them to others? Compliments cost nothing, but a genuine compliment can brighten someone's day and make them feel good. Do you find it easier to give other people compliments than yourself? Start with that. Observe what you like about someone and when you are ready, choose to share it.

4. Receive compliments. Dating is one of the environments in which you are likely to receive a compliment. Practising how to respond can therefore pay off. Compliments are like gifts. Can you imagine turning down a gift and throwing it back in someone's face? Then don't turn down a compliment. Just smile and say, 'Thank you.' Even if you don't agree or feel embarrassed, practise saying 'thank you' for the other person.

5. Use your body. A massive 55 per cent of communication comes from our body language. How we hold and use our bodies determines whether we give out positive or negative signals. Observe confident people. Look at how they hold themselves. They walk tall and with ease, regardless of their height. Their heads are held high and they look directly at people.

Spend time observing how you walk and hold yourself. Don't be critical, be constructive. Concentrate on maintaining 'open' body language, making eye contact and smiling at people.

Key idea

It's the relationships you have the confidence to walk away from that create the space for new ones to come along.

6

Preparing to Fly

Make the most of yourself, for that is all there is of you

RALPH WALDO EMERSON

ARE YOU READY?

There is a difference between wishing for something and being ready for it. You might have been wishing for a date for years but haven't done anything to prepare for it or indicate to others that you're interested.

> If you are ready to meet someone, don't keep it a secret. Let friends and work colleagues know that you are open to meeting people

I often found myself saying to friends, 'I don't really have the time to meet a man at the moment, I'm so busy,' and yet I was convinced I was open to meeting someone. So the invites to parties or gatherings where I might meet someone were not particularly forthcoming as everyone thought I'd be too busy!

Take a look at your diary; are you too busy to meet someone? Do you find yourself giving friends the message that you have no time? If so, you could be reducing the possibilities of that happening.

GIVE UP ON FATE

Take off any rose-coloured spectacles you might be wearing. Hoping that fate will take its course and you'll meet the love of your life is unrealistic.

One of my clients, a very successful senior manager in a blue-chip company, came to me because she was having no luck in finding love. In talking to her, I discovered that she held the belief that when the time was right a relationship would come along. She believed in the idea that if it was meant to be, she would meet someone, perhaps in a supermarket queue or maybe through a client at work. However, holding on to these beliefs and hopes was not helping her. Leaving things to chance and hoping a man would magically appear one day had not produced any results and she was ready to try a different approach.

I pointed out that she owed her success in her career to the fact that she had not left things to chance. She had taken action, ensuring that she got to know the right people, let them know she was interested in furthering her career, taking courses and generally getting herself noticed.

I explained that if she had applied the same belief to her career as she was doing to finding love, then she would still be on the first rung of the ladder. The penny dropped and we constructed a plan of action. Five months later, she was dating a wonderful man whom she'd met through placing an advert in a lonely hearts column.

The truth of the matter is that if you want to meet someone, you will have to put yourself in situations where you come into contact with potential dates. Dating is a numbers game: the more people you go out with, the greater your chances of finding someone with whom you connect. Also, the more you date, the more finely tuned your instincts will become. Instead of hoping that you will find love, make a commitment to yourself that you *will* find love.

BE DETERMINED TO SUCCEED

Dating can be fun; it can also be tedious and boring. You may have to go on many dates before you find love. However, unless you decide that you have the commitment and determination to succeed then you might not last the course. Make that decision now.

Answer the following by giving a score out of ten where one is not at all and ten is extremely.

- How determined are you to find love?
- How committed are you to keep going until you find love?

If you scored seven or below for either of these, ask yourself what it would take to move your score to an eight or above.

When you have your answer, go ahead and take whatever steps are necessary to increase your determination or commitment. If finding love is important to you then make it a high priority.

BUT DO YOUR RESEARCH!

What options are available in your area to meet potential dates? Do some research before you decide which are for you. Find out what is involved, what the costs are and if this might appeal to you. Asking others is fine, but the answer you get may depend upon their experience or success, and what suits one person does not always suit another. The only way to tell is to find out for yourself; be your own best judge.

INTERNET DATING

This is becoming an extremely popular way of meeting people. I know many clients and friends who have met their partners through Internet dating sites and without Internet dating I would never have met my fiancé Tony. Of course you will always hear of stories of married men or women who only want to use sites to have affairs. To avoid this happening, on my profile I added, 'Thank you to those of you who respond but please don't bother if you are a smoker, are still married or going out with someone.' In my experience being upfront and honest pays off and can help avoid attracting people who are unavailable.

Internet Dating Tips

- Look around before choosing your Internet dating site. Choose one that gives more than just the basic details about its members. Extra information that can give you a better idea about someone includes their favourite social activities, personal characteristics, foods liked, magazines or papers read

- Post a recent photo of yourself, looking good. You'll get more responses with a photo than without. Most people will look at the photos before the profiles so make sure yours is a good one!

- Don't start an e-mail relationship with someone until you have seen their photo. Let's face it, if you don't fancy them it will save a lot of time-wasting!

- Answer all messages (except those that are offensive). It's not only polite, but it will be good practice for turning anyone down gently on a real date

- Avoid using a sexually provocative online name and avoid sex talk in general. That is if you are serious about finding love

- Beware, there are people on these sites who are happy to chat to you online but will never ask you out. They are cyber-daters, i.e. chatting online is all they are interested in. If after a few e-mails you indicate that you are interested in speaking to them or meeting them for real and they do not take the hint, move on

- Arrange to have a chat on the phone before going

on a real date. If you don't like the sound of someone's voice then a date will be a non-starter. If you are looking for a long-term relationship, you are going to have to hear that voice for a long time so it's important that it's pleasant to listen to

• Apply the normal safety rules for dating even if you have got to know the person well via the Internet

SPEED DATING

This is one of the newest imports from the US and is catching on in Europe. Speed dating is great for those who don't have much time on their hands. It's an opportunity to meet lots of people in a short space of time and find out if you like someone enough to meet them again.

If you usually know within the first few minutes of talking to someone if there is an attraction, then this could be worth trying. It's probably more suited to those who are fairly confident, as there's no room for preamble. You have just a few minutes to meet each person, get to know them, have them get to know you and decide whether you'd like to get to know them a little bit more!

At the end of the allotted time, the man moves

to another table while the woman stays put and you both mark down on cards whether you would like to see one another again.

At the end of the evening, the cards are collected and if two of you have ticked each other, then the organisers will provide you both with each other's e-mail addresses. The rest is up to you!

Tips for Speed Dating

- First impressions count, so even if you're in your work clothes, take extra care over your appearance. Wear something that will make you feel confident
- Smile and make eye contact – you've only got a short time in which to make a good impression and this is one of the quickest ways to do this
- Plan in advance some unusual questions to ask rather than where do you live or what do you do for a living. Some speed dating events actually ban the use of these questions. (See the section on open questions for some suggestions)

INTRODUCTION AGENCIES

There are a wide range of introduction agencies offering different types of service. These agencies normally vet their clients and many offer a personal service where they interview each client and then find them a suitable match. However, there are no guarantees.

Introduction agencies usually attract the more mature client from the age of thirty-plus. Of all the dating options, they are by and large the most expensive. However, because they are pricey, their members tend to be serious about wanting a long-term relationship.

Tips for Introduction Agencies

- Contact a few agencies before making your choice so that you are aware of the range of services they provide
- Ask how many people in your age range they currently have on their books. Some agencies will allow you to look through a selection of profiles in your introductory visit
- Ask whether they guarantee a certain number of introductions for your fee
- Ask if you can freeze your membership. This is very useful if you start dating someone and four months down the line the relationship ends: it means you have not lost out on four months of membership

- Be specific about what type of person you want to meet. The more idea they have of what you are or are not looking for, the more chance you have of them finding a good match

COURSES, EVENTS OR CLUBS

Less targeted but still effective places to meet people are courses, events or clubs where you have a chance to socialise with other participants. I have known many friends and clients who met their partners through taking part in activities they enjoy or want to learn. They include: self-development courses; reiki courses; foreign language classes; salsa classes; amateur dramatics groups; fun runs; and charity walks.

The list of possible courses and events is endless. Meeting someone at these events is of course never guaranteed. However, as long as you have an opportunity to meet the participants in a social setting and the event or class is well attended the potential is always there.

To increase your chances, you need to be proactive at these events. If there are people you would like to meet again or you have got on well with, don't rely on someone asking you to join them for lunch or a drink afterwards. Take the lead and ask others to join you. Be the one to organise a meal or a picnic or a party for everyone. If there is someone you are attracted to but are too scared to ask out, inviting them to a group event is a great way of seeing them again.

Always bear in mind that even though you may not meet the love of your life at these events, they could provide opportunities to extend your social circle. This is especially important if you have been stuck in a social rut and are not meeting anyone new.

> To increase your chances you need to be proactive

THE ART OF SMALL TALK

There's no getting away from it: if you want to meet someone then at some stage you will have to engage in small talk. Put any negative thoughts you may have about small talk to one side and consider the benefits. Small talk is the very thing that allows you to get to know someone. It's also the very thing that establishes friendships and relationships. Perfecting the art of small talk can open up endless possibilities for meeting people and the potential to find love.

The two most basic skills you need are the skills that you have been using all your life: questioning and listening. The art of small talk involves developing these skills in such a way that you can start and keep a conversation going. Here are some techniques you can apply.

Open Up the Conversation

Open questions are great for starting and continuing conversations because they require the person answering to provide more than a 'yes' or 'no' answer. For example:

- How was your journey?
- How do you know Sue and Peter?
- How are you finding this dating agency?

Keep It Going

There are some topics that are easier to talk about than others, and when engaging in small talk the aim is to keep the conversation as light and easy as possible. Topics that are easy to develop a conversation around include: travel, food, restaurants, places to visit, films and music. In fact as long as the topic you pick is fairly upbeat, you can talk about virtually anything. And by asking more of those open questions you have a better chance of developing the conversation and keeping it going. Open questions usually begin with: what, how, why, who or where. Here's the advantage of using open as opposed to closed questions:

Q. *Do you like Indian food?*
A. *Yes, do you?*
A. *Yes.*
Q. *Have you been to India?*
A. *No.*

Hopefully a conversation would not be that stilted even if you did use closed questions. But asking open questions is far more effective:

Tom: *What types of food do you enjoy eating?*
Sue: *I love Indian, Thai, Italian, French. How about you?*
Tom: *I really enjoy Indian too. I've never been to India but I'd love to go, I love travelling. I've just come back from Thailand.*
Sue: *How wonderful. What was that like?*

Notice in the above example, even though Tom did not ask Sue another question, she was able to use what he had been talking about to keep the conversation going by asking an open question. Here are some suggestions:

- Which area/place did you enjoy visiting most?
- What made you decide to join/visit?
- What initially attracted you to the work that you do?
- What do you enjoy most about travelling/your job?
- What does that involve?

Sometimes it's not easy to converse with people who do not reciprocate by asking us questions. You can often get them to continue by saying, 'That sounds interesting, tell me more about that.'

Be an Active Listener

Listening is a skill that many take for granted. However, it can make the difference between creating a good or a bad impression. Active listening, as the name suggests, involves a response to show the person that you're listening. This can be achieved in several ways:

- Making eye contact, looking into the eyes of the person you are talking to and letting your eyes

convey positive messages, such as, 'That's fascinating, touching, amusing'
- Giving the occasional nod, combined with a few 'aha's and 'mmm's
- Using words that show that you are interested in what's being said, such as, 'Really!' 'That's good', 'I'm amazed', 'Fascinating'
- Listening for possible links or areas of shared interest, repeating these and using them to move the conversation on. For example, 'You've just come back from Thailand, I would love to go there. What was your favourite part?'

Be Genuinely Interested

When it comes to making a good impression, however, one of the most appealing characteristics you can develop is to be genuinely interested in others.

In the dating stakes, showing interest in another person's day, their thoughts, hopes, dreams and aspirations will definitely win you brownie points.

Try it out in everyday situations with a variety of people. Don't just treat it as an exercise; remember, it's about showing a sincere interest in someone's life. You could ask:

- How has your week gone?
- What are you most looking forward to doing at the weekend?
- Where are you going on your holidays this year?

Asking these kinds of questions and listening with interest to the answer will allow you to gain practice in being attentive.

Don't Interrupt

Many people do this without realising it, but unfortunately it's one of the least helpful things you can do when you're trying to make a good impression. People often jump in too quickly when they are excited or nervous. But interrupting someone can give the impression that you are not interested in what they are saying.

And Don't 'Go One Better'

Negating someone else's experience or going one better than them is another behaviour that people are sometimes unaware of. A couple I overheard recently brought this home to me. The woman had experienced an awful day by the sounds of it, but instead of listening and empathising, the man chose to share his day with her. He probably thought he was telling her that he knew what it was like to have a bad day. However, it did not come across like that. It was more like, 'You think you've had a bad day, mine was much worse!'

Using an opportunity to recount how your experience was far worse or much more exciting than someone else's is a real conversation killer. A person's experience or story is important to them. Respecting that, even if you're not particularly interested in it, is one of the keys to the art of small talk.

FIRST IMPRESSIONS COUNT

There is no getting away from it, first impressions count. However, there are some things that you can practise beforehand so that by the time you go on a date they have become second nature:

- Smile: practise a genuine warm smile that invites a person to get to know you better
- Sound enthusiastic and interested: observe, or, better still, ask a trusted friend to observe your voice and give you feedback on whether you sound enthusiastic or interested
- Engage in eye contact: practise this as often as

you can until you become comfortable with making and sustaining eye contact

- Practise asking easy-to-answer, open, non-threatening questions
- Learn to pay genuine compliments: if you don't do this naturally, practise noticing something positive about the person you are with and pay them a genuine compliment
- Practise active listening
- Use positive language: avoid making negative comments or criticisms about people and places, the restaurant, food and so on

PRACTISE ASKING FOR A DATE

If you are a man, practise asking a woman out aloud in the comfort of your own home. If you are nervous, practise what to say until you sound confident. Use closed questions for this – after all, you are looking for a definite answer!

For example, 'Would you like to meet for a coffee or a drink?' Do not add some time to this question. Follow it up with; 'When are you free?'

It may seem a little old-fashioned but it is still true that many men, particularly older ones, prefer to ask rather than be asked. That said, it can be a burden having to make the running all the time and some men really appreciate women making the effort. This is not clear-cut territory so it pays to use your instincts.

Another option is to let the other person know of an event you might both enjoy or invite them to a party where there will be other people so that they don't feel under pressure.

THE WORK

1. Make a commitment. Make a commitment to yourself that you will make a continued effort to meet people and go on dates until you find love.

2. Just do it! Joining a club, an Internet dating site or placing an ad in a lonely hearts column isn't enough. You have to turn up, chat to people and be proactive, otherwise it's like joining a gym, never going and then wondering why you're not getting fit. Decide what you are going to do and do it!

3. Develop your curiosity. If you tend to dry up when it comes to asking questions, developing a natural curiosity about people is a great way to overcome this. Start by using the words 'I wonder'. Then, think of all the things you wonder about someone.

For example, I wonder what he likes to do at week-ends? I wonder what food or music she likes? I wonder what he does for a living? I wonder if she likes dogs?

This is an ideal exercise when sitting in a pavement café watching the world go by. Observe the things you wonder about a person. Then use this sense of curiosity to turn your wonder into questions: What music do you like listening to? What do you enjoy doing at weekends?

4. Look for possible venues. Be prepared to suggest some suitable venues for a date, but do visit them beforehand. Knowing where they are and whether you can hold a conversation without being drowned out by loud music can help you to feel more comfortable and therefore confident on a date.

5. Date safely. The dating safety precautions are usually intended for women, but it is important that everyone dates safely and it is useful for a man to be aware of these so that he can help his date to feel comfortable.

- Arrange to meet in a public place
- Do not leave your drink unattended as this makes you vulnerable to 'spiking' with date rape drugs

- Do not drink excessive amounts of alcohol
- Do not ask the person back to your place
- If you feel at all uncomfortable or threatened at any time during a date, excuse yourself and leave
- Let a friend know where you are going and what time you will be home

Key idea

Preparation is the key to success; you never get a second chance to make a first impression.

7

Sustaining Momentum

If you really want to do something, you'll find a way; if you don't, you'll find an excuse

ANON

To achieve your goal it's important to keep trying. Sustaining momentum is one of the hardest steps en route to finding love. It's sometimes not easy to keep up the effort required and that's exactly what it takes, effort, when time after time you meet people who are just 'not right' for you. However it is precisely at those points when you feel frustrated or discouraged that you need to sustain the momentum.

REKINDLE THE FLAME

> The only way you can fail is if you give up

Get back in touch with what you really want and take another look at how important this is to you. Reread your journal. Look over all the exercises you've completed detailing the reasons why you want a relationship. Get out that wish list and start up those daydreams!

Go to see a romantic film. These can be great motivators, helping to remind you that you want to find love.

If you've got to the stage where you think, There is no one out there that I fancy, spend an evening looking on the Internet dating sites. There are literally thousands of people on some of these sites. If you are looking for a Brad Pitt or Jennifer Aniston look-alike you may have a challenge on your hands. But even if you're very choosy, if you keep looking you will find someone who catches your eye. This will help to reinforce the belief that, 'There are men that I fancy.'

If finding love is important to you then don't give up. Take a break, focus on something else for a while, but don't give up on your goal. The only way you can fail is if you give up.

TAKE OUT THE WHYS

When things seem to be taking longer than anticipated and everyone around you seems to have a partner, the 'why' questions tend to creep in. Why haven't I met anyone yet? Why have I not been successful when I've put in so much effort? Why have all my friends found someone and not me? Why can't I find someone?

Asking yourself 'why?' will keep you going around in circles. It will also take your focus away from what will move you forward. If you want to analyse the reasons why, then ask yourself in a more productive way. For example: 'What might be the reasons for me not being successful or finding someone?' Then follow this up with: 'So what am I going to do about it?'

Thinking what you can do about your current situation and then taking action will help you to get what you want, not asking 'why?'

COPING WITH REJECTION

It's an inevitable fact of dating that at some stage you are going to have to deal with rejection. It's worth remembering, though, that it's the gaps that are created by the break-up of relationships that provide the space for the 'right' relationship to come along.

One of the keys to dealing with rejection is to realise that it is not really you as an entity that is being rejected. Dating is a screening process and each person has a set of criteria which are unknown to other people. In the past, you may have found yourself dismissing someone because they smoked; had the wrong accent; were too short, too tall, too fat, too thin, too loud and so on. In other words they did not meet your criteria.

No matter what you look like, what you do for a living or how wonderful you are, at some point, probably at many points, you are going to be rejected. Something, be it a physical characteristic that you do or don't have, what you wear, or, for example, the fact that you love dogs, is going to be enough to make someone reject you because you don't meet *their* criteria. This is nothing personal, it's not about you; it's about them and the criteria they are using.

For example, it might be that you smoke and they don't want to date a smoker, or that you're small and they prefer taller people. Learning not to analyse rejection but rather to accept it for what it is – simply that you don't meet that person's criteria – allows you to move on to find someone who does appreciate you for who you are.

Dust Yourself Down

Coping with rejection is like riding a horse: every once in a while you fall off and the best thing you can do is dust yourself down, climb back on and start all over again

Just like falling off a horse, rejection hurts but that's no reason to wallow in self-pity. Analysing what went wrong or what someone didn't like about you, is largely unproductive. You can go round and round in circles looking for the hidden meanings in things. The next person you choose to date is going to have an entirely new set of criteria anyway, so you'll be in the same boat again. Unless you're a mind-reader, you'll never be able to predict what someone's looking for.

Remember, you are wonderful. You are unique. You have lots of great qualities and if someone doesn't appreciate you for who you are, they are not the one for you. It doesn't matter if all the people you've met so far cannot handle being with someone who is an extrovert or an introvert. You are only looking for one who can.

TAKE A BREAK

Dating can be very demanding. I know from personal experience and that of my clients that you may find yourself wondering if you can continue to make the effort. So, if you have reached the stage where your enthusiasm for dating is starting to wane, take a break.

If your focus has been on finding a partner and you're tired of making an effort, take the pressure off the accelerator for a while. Do whatever it takes to recharge your batteries. Concentrate on you rather than on finding someone else. Go and do something that's fun, enjoyable, something different.

Taking a break can be beneficial when it comes to finding love. And as a fantastic side effect, giving yourself some time out can sometimes produce great results! I know of many instances where people have met their partners at that very moment, just when they least expected it and when they weren't even looking.

It's important, however, not to hold on to the expectation that 'something might happen'. Taking a break means just that. So whatever you choose to do, drop any thoughts of meeting someone. Concentrate on enjoying yourself.

What would help you to have a complete break from dating and recharge your batteries? There are some wonderful activity holidays available now: painting in Tuscany; improving your culinary skills in a French château; rambling in Andalusia; horse riding in Tibet; yoga in Greece; poetry writing in Provence; the list is endless. If money is a concern, then there are many short courses available to help take your mind off things.

Activity holidays are quite different from singles holidays. The focus of an activity holiday is to learn a new skill or take part in an activity you enjoy. If you happen to make friends or meet someone, then that's a bonus.

CREATE A SUPPORT TEAM

It's sometimes difficult to sustain enthusiasm for continued effort on your own, so create a support team. This can consist of any number of trusted people who are willing to support you in your goal of finding love.

One essential role is that of a person who can help you to stay objective. Often when dating our emotions take over and can distort reality. Help from an objective and trusted friend can be a valuable asset when dating to ensure that your emotions do not cloud your judgement.

A good role model is another valuable team member, someone who is experiencing what you are looking for – a great relationship. Spending time in the company of this person or couple can be a great learning opportunity. For example, if you have grown up in a dysfunctional family and have no idea what it means to have a successful relationship, you can learn from someone who does. You might want to have several team members who fulfil this role so that you get different perspectives. It also means that you have constant exposure to the fact that successful relationships are possible.

The final members of your team need to be those who can cheer you up when you've been rejected. People who will pick you up when you're down, take you out and remind you that life is fun.

The good news is that you don't even need to approach people or let them know that they are members of your team – apart from the person who provides an objective sounding board. The others can simply be people you are acquainted with anyway. All you have to do is to cultivate and maintain your relationships with them and ask for their support in whatever form you need when required.

EXPERIMENT

If you treat dating like an experiment, then there are no wrong moves. You can't get it wrong because the purpose of an experiment is simply to find out if a particular method works or not. If it doesn't, you observe what happened and try a slightly different approach in the next experiment.

Listen to your internal language. Are you saying to yourself, 'I should have done this,' or, 'I shouldn't have done that'? Judging or criticising yourself is counter-productive. Similarly, check whether you are blaming other people for your lack of success. The sorts of things I hear from time to time are, 'If my friends invited other single people to their parties I might meet someone,' or, 'If she'd suggested another date then I would have gone out with her again.'

Take responsibility for creating what you want to happen. Ask friends to invite single people to their parties. In fact, ask your friends to ask their friends to invite as many single people along as possible!

> Take responsibility for creating what you want to happen

If you want another date with someone, then suggest something they might like to see or do, or tell them about an event that's coming up and invite them along.

DYNAMIC DECISION-MAKING

Clients often say to me, 'I'm afraid of making the wrong decision.' Decisions in dating need to be made all the time: the decision to ask someone out or accept a date; the decision to go on another date or form a relationship, and so on. So where could you possibly make what you might consider the 'wrong' decision?

At the beginning of the dating process, asking someone out or accepting an invitation, you are in 'exploratory mode'. The challenge comes when you need to decide whether to suggest or accept another date, to develop or continue the relationship.

The more attention you pay at the beginning of the dating process or relationship, the greater your chances of success.

Deciding to Continue

Here are three simple questions to ask yourself to help you to decide whether to continue:

1. Do I like this person?
2. Do I want to spend more time with them?
3. How do they make me feel?

I have found that for many clients, the focus tends to be more on what the other person thought of them and how they themselves came across on the date.

After several years of unsuccessful dating Rita came to me for coaching. In the past she had been so focused on getting a date and ultimately a relationship that she had not examined how *she* felt. In her words she was 'just grateful to be in a relationship'. Rita recognised that this was not helping her to get what she wanted. Once she had gained some clarity on exactly what she did want, I set her the challenge of listening to her inner voice, taking notice of those feelings and paying attention to any inner dialogue.

She learned to give up the expectation that 'this might be the one' and began to pay attention to her date and how she felt about spending time with him. Rita reported an almost immediate change. She noticed that by paying attention to answering the three questions, she was able to take a much more objective view of the date. It also enabled her to stop feeling as self-conscious and she was able to relax a lot more.

Decision-making is one of the keys to successful dating. Be honest with yourself from the very beginning. Why would you go out for a second date with someone whose company you didn't enjoy or who didn't make you feel good?

In a relationship, decision-making is constantly evolving. It's a dynamic process. We need to evaluate our decisions continually, based on the information we have. As you get to know someone, keep asking yourself the three questions. If the answers to 'Do I like this person?' and 'Do I want to spend more time with this person' become 'No' or 'Not really', then it's time to move on.

Remember, it's the relationships you walk away from that create the space for the 'good ones' to come along.

KEEP AN OPEN MIND

This message is directed to everyone reading this who is tempted to give up because the person they like has not called them.

You have given out what you think are lots of clues that you're interested. You may even have given the person your telephone number and suggested they give you a call. But so far they haven't. At this point, despite your inclination, don't give up. Keep your options open. There may be a perfectly genuine reason as to why they have not called.

This doesn't mean you have to sit by the phone, not go out with anyone else or take a break from dating. Carry on with your normal life. Put any disappointment to one side and in the words of the song think, *Que sera, sera* – what will be will be.

So many women I know give up when a man does not appear to show interest immediately. Men too, for that matter. The mind kicks in and feeds you all sorts of assumptions: 'Well, if he's not going to phone then he can't be interested.' Keeping the door open means not judging the person for not phoning or contacting you as frequently as you would like.

I know this one's really tough, but applying the '*que sera, sera*' approach and refusing to be judgemental can pay dividends. I would not have met my fiancé Tony if I had not applied this principle.

Early on in our Internet encounters Tony asked me if I had any free slots in my diary for a chat. It was three months down the line before this actually happened! If I had made the assumption that he wasn't interested and had not kept an open mind we would both have missed out on a wonderful relationship.

What did I do? Well, I applied my principle, kept

an open dialogue with Tony whenever we were online and in the meantime went out with other men! In other words, I was open to the possibility that nothing would happen with Tony. However, I was also open to the possibility that we might meet eventually and either become friends or something more. Needless to say it paid off!

In our online conversations we would sometimes ask one another how we were getting along with the Internet dating site. I was absolutely honest with Tony in that I let him know when I was going out on a date with someone. It was this that finally made the difference. He sent me an e-mail asking how one date had gone. Unfortunately his e-mail had been delivered into my junk mail folder and I only empty this once in a while. He sent two more, but as I wasn't aware of them, I did not reply.

Several weeks later we were online at the same time. He asked me how my date had gone. He thought, because I had not replied to his e-mails, that I'd been 'taken'. That same night he finally asked me out – it was Valentine's Day.

My point in sharing this with you is not to flag up my experience as an example to follow. It's simply to say that remaining open can pay real dividends.

If finding love is really important to you, then

don't give up, keep an open mind and keep going until you find it.

> Whatever your age, it's never too late to find love

THE WORK

1. Why keep going? If you have got to the stage where dating seems to be a chore or if your enthusiasm is waning, take time to answer the question, 'Why is this important to me?' Reminding yourself why you are making this effort can help sustain the momentum.

2. Expand your horizons. Be prepared to try many different approaches to find love. Don't be too quick to dismiss things. Just because one singles holiday or one speed dating event didn't work for you doesn't mean to say another might not. Of course everyone has different tastes so I'm not saying keep going along to things you don't like, but don't tar similar events with the same brush.

3. Find solutions. As people's lives have become busier and more work-centred, the amount of time many can devote to meeting someone is limited. There are so many different ways of meeting people now that it is possible to find methods that do fit into your schedule. Make a decision to find a solution that works for you.

4. Review your progress. To help you to sustain momentum, write down the progress that you've made. This may be progress in your levels of confidence when dating, progress in chatting to people, progress in making decisions or saying goodbye to relationships that are not right for you.

Take a moment now to find answers to complete these three sentences with as many different endings as you can and write them down in your journal.

- I am good at...................
- I am now better at ....
- I still want to improve upon.............

For example:

- I am good at listening on a date
- I am now better at making eye contact
- I still want to improve upon my body language so that I appear more confident and attractive to the opposite sex

5. **Be happy.** If finding love is important to you, do whatever it takes for however long it takes, but in the meantime concentrate on being happy. Being happy in the present is the greatest gift you can give yourself and the greatest preparation for successful dating. When you find happiness with yourself then you will find happiness with another. Give yourself a daily dose by spending just five minutes thinking of all the things that have brought you happiness during the day. Notice what they are and become more aware of them as time goes by. Don't seek happiness – create it!

Key idea

When you find happiness with yourself then you will find happiness with another.

I wish you great luck on your journey . . .

**Transform your life
with Hodder Mobius**

For the latest information on the best in
Spirituality, Self-Help,
Health & Wellbeing and Parenting,

visit our website
www.hoddermobius.com